Your Start-Up Starts Now!
A Guide to Entrepreneurship

What Is Entrepreneurship?

Natalie Hyde

Author: Natalie Hyde

Series research and development: Reagan Miller

Editors: Rosemary Quinsey, Kathy Middleton

Proofreader: Kelly Stern

Editorial services: Clarity Content Services

Project coordinator and prepress technician: Tammy McGarr

Print coordinator: Katherine Berti

Series consultant: Rebecca Darling

Cover design: Margaret Amy Salter

Design: David Montle

Photo Research: Linda Tanaka

Photo Credits:

Cover: All images from Shutterstock
Title page: SpeedKingz/Shutterstock; p4 Gordon Bell/Shutterstock; p5 Hershey Community Archives; p6 CCL/Michiel Hendryckx; p7 Chubykin Arkady/Shutterstock; p8 stefanolunardi/Shutterstock; p9 Larry St. Pierre/Shutterstock; p10 Benoit Daoust/Shutterstock; p11 Daniel M Ernst/Shutterstock; p12 Public Domain; p13 LesPalenik/Shutterstock; p14 Sheila Fitzgerald/Shutterstock; p15 SvedOliver/Shutterstock; p16 Rawpixel/Shutterstock; p17 top kgelati/Shutterstock, Courtesy of Chad Mureta; p18 Tarapong Siri/Shutterstock, Eva Katalin Kondoros/iStock; p20 Courtesy of Andrew Hall and Jeremy Bryant, Mealshare; p21 Khakimullin Aleksandr/Shutterstock; p22 Marius Pirvu/Shutterstock; p23 Odua Images/Shutterstock; p25 left goodluz/Shutterstock, SergeBertasiusPhotography/Shutterstock, pixs4u/Shutterstock, stockyimages/Shutterstock, StockLite/Shutterstock; p26 Courtesy of George Vlagos; p27 Everett-Art/Shutterstock; p28 sindlera/Shutterstock; p29 Kinga/Shutterstock, Rawpixel.com/Shutterstock; p30 Burlingham/Shutterstock; p31 Courtesy of Liz Forkin Bohannon/Sseko Design; p32 left 360b/Shutterstock, tanuha2001/Shutterstock, McDonald's; p34 Pojoslaw/dreamstime; p35 top Courtesy of April Glavine, Robert Johns/Alamy; p36 Frank Anusewicz/Shutterstock; p37 Courtesy of Naturalicious; p39 Monkey Business Images/Shutterstock; p40 George Rudy/Shutterstock; p41 top Photographer Annabella Charles. Used by permission of Moziah Bridges, Photo courtesy of Juliette Brindak Blake; p42 Ralwel/Shutterstock.

t=Top, bl=Bottom Left, br=Bottom Right

Library and Archives Canada Cataloguing in Publication

Hyde, Natalie, 1963-, author
What is entrepreneurship? / Natalie Hyde.

(Your start-up starts now! a guide to entrepreneurship)
Includes bibliographical references and index.
Issued in print and electronic formats.
ISBN 978-0-7787-2766-8 (paperback).--
ISBN 978-0-7787-2758-3 (hardback).--
ISBN 978-1-4271-1824-0 (html)

1. New business enterprises--Juvenile literature.
2. Entrepreneurship--Juvenile literature. 3. Small business--Juvenile literature. I. Title.

HD62.5.H94 2016 j658.1'1 C2016-903423-2
C2016-903424-0

Library of Congress Cataloging-in-Publication Data

Names: Hyde, Natalie, 1963- author.
Title: What is entrepreneurship? / Natalie Hyde.
Description: New York : Crabtree Publishing, [2017] |
Series: Your start-up starts now! A guide to entrepreneurship |
Includes bibliographical references and index.
Identifiers: LCCN 2016026651 (print) | LCCN 2016038422 (ebook) |
ISBN 9780778727583 (reinforced library binding) |
ISBN 9780778727668 (pbk.) |
ISBN 9781427118240 (Electronic HTML)
Subjects: LCSH: Entrepreneurship--Juvenile literature. | New business enterprises--Juvenile literature.
Classification: LCC HB615 .H966 2017 (print) | LCC HB615 (ebook) |
DDC 658.1/1--dc23
LC record available at https://lccn.loc.gov/2016026651

Crabtree Publishing Company
www.crabtreebooks.com 1-800-387-7650

Printed in Canada/102016/IH20160811

Published in Canada
Crabtree Publishing
616 Welland Ave.
St. Catharines, Ontario
L2M 5V6

Published in the United States
Crabtree Publishing
PMB 59051
350 Fifth Avenue, 59th Floor
New York, New York 10118

Published in the United Kingdom
Crabtree Publishing
Maritime House
Basin Road North, Hove
BN41 1WR

Published in Australia
Crabtree Publishing
3 Charles Street
Coburg North
VIC, 3058

Contents

If at First You Don't Succeed...

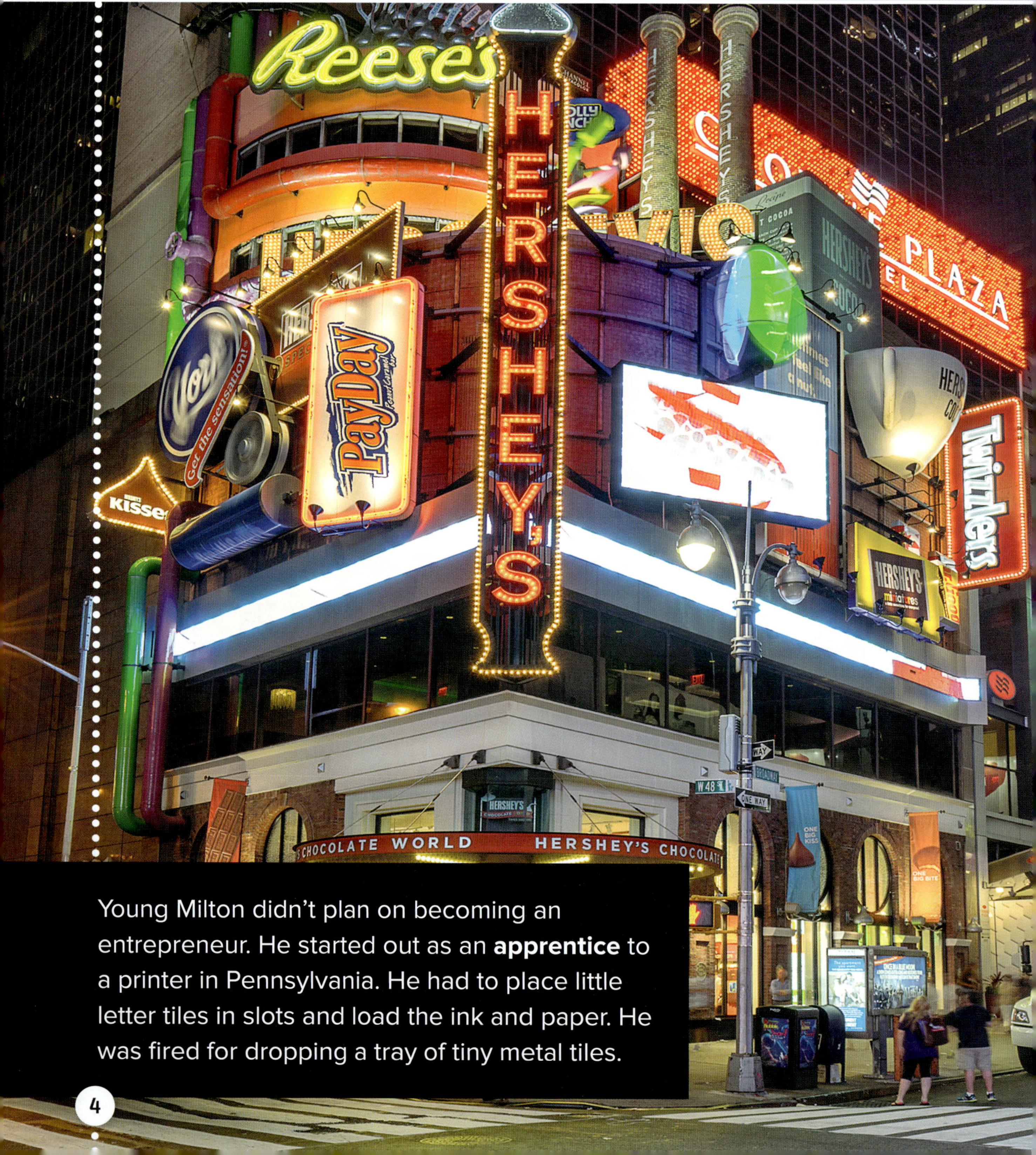

Young Milton didn't plan on becoming an entrepreneur. He started out as an **apprentice** to a printer in Pennsylvania. He had to place little letter tiles in slots and load the ink and paper. He was fired for dropping a tray of tiny metal tiles.

Milton Hershey built one of the biggest chocolate companies in the world.

Next, Milton became an apprentice in a candy-making factory. At the age of 19, Milton left his position to start his own candy company. Like many entrepreneurs, he had to start small. He borrowed money from his uncle and sold taffy and caramels from a pushcart. After making very little money for six years, he closed the business.

Milton then moved to Chicago and opened another candy business. This time he experimented by adding fresh milk to chocolate. But this business failed, too.

Determined to succeed, he moved to New York City and opened yet another small business. But the price of sugar was high. It made his chocolates cost too much to make, and he went **bankrupt**.

Milton went home to Pennsylvania. He scraped money together once again and started the Lancaster Caramel Company. He used fresh milk to make "Hershey's Crystal A" caramels. Finally, this candy was a success. Milton Hershey went on to become one of the biggest names in candy-making history.

Milton Hershey displayed some of the qualities that are essential for entrepreneurs: determination, flexibility, and hard work. But why does someone want to become be an entrepreneur?

Entrepreneurs

- follow their passion—Imagine making a living doing something you enjoy!
- change the world—If you see a problem, use your skills to create a solution.
- help the **economy**—Support your community by creating jobs.
- control their destiny—You can be in charge of your own life.

"My experience has shown me that the people who are exceptionally good in business aren't so because of what they know, but because of their **insatiable** need to know more."

—Milton Hershey

1 What Is an Entrepreneur?

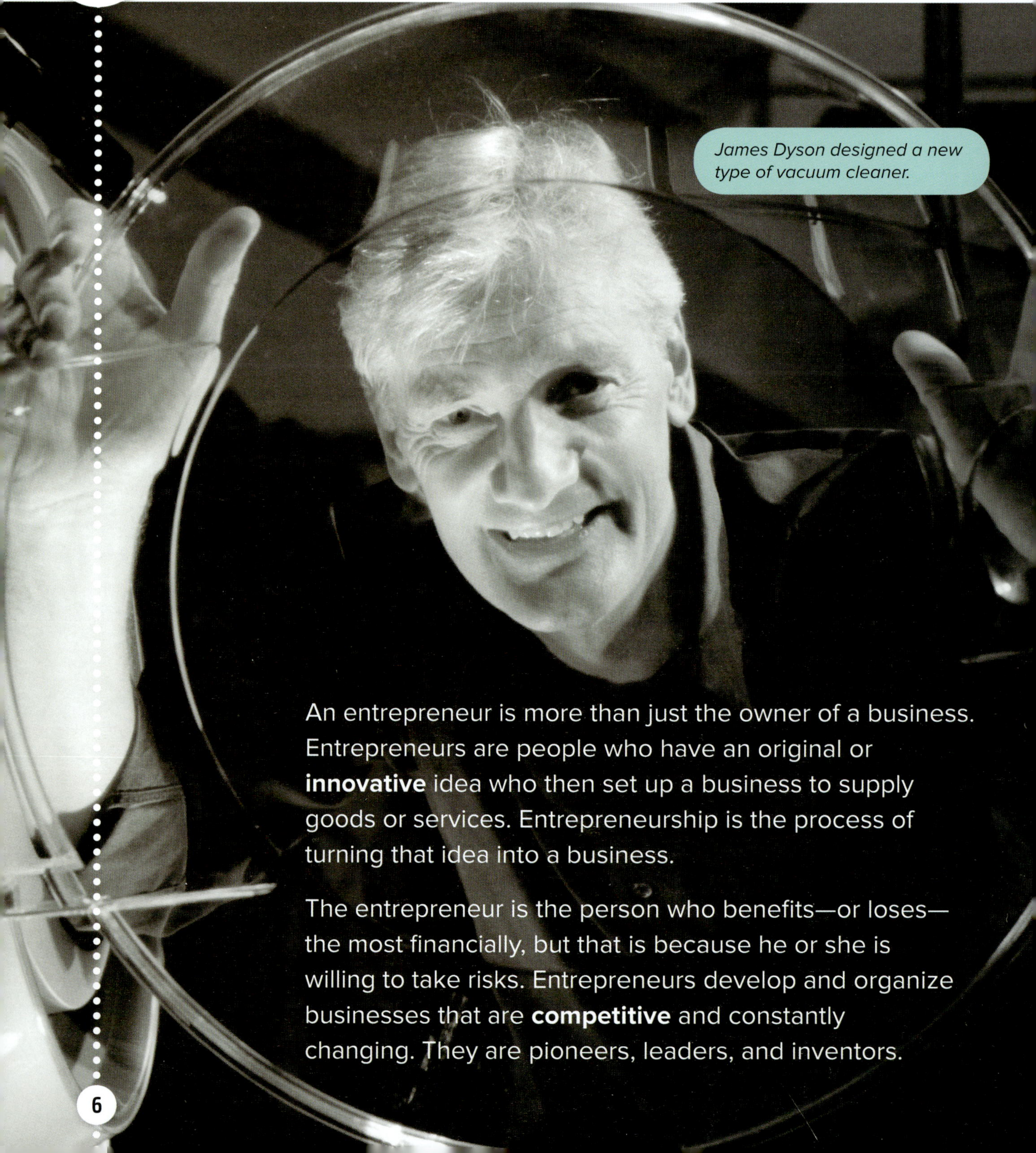

James Dyson designed a new type of vacuum cleaner.

An entrepreneur is more than just the owner of a business. Entrepreneurs are people who have an original or **innovative** idea who then set up a business to supply goods or services. Entrepreneurship is the process of turning that idea into a business.

The entrepreneur is the person who benefits—or loses—the most financially, but that is because he or she is willing to take risks. Entrepreneurs develop and organize businesses that are **competitive** and constantly changing. They are pioneers, leaders, and inventors.

Dreamers

It is passion that drives entrepreneurs to succeed. Steve Jobs is an example of someone who had a dream of making the best personal computer available. He started Apple Computer and changed technology forever.

Mark Zuckerberg wanted to create a way for students at his college to connect and share online. He created something called "theFacebook." This soon grew into the social media site we know as Facebook, which has more than a billion users.

Both of these entrepreneurs focused on their goal and created change. Whether it leads to a new product or a new service, a person's passion is what determines the type of business they pursue.

James Dyson: Founder of Dyson Ltd.

James Dyson found vacuuming a chore. The machine didn't move smoothly, and he hated changing the messy bag. He thought using a ball instead of a wheel would help the machine move in a more flexible way. He also reused an idea he had to make better fans to remove dust in sawmills and developed a new type of bagless vacuum cleaner. His machine became the best-selling vacuum in the United Kingdom in just 18 months.

While all entrepreneurs follow similar steps in creating a business, it is passion that often defines what field of entrepreneurship they will enter. Different types of entrepreneurs include the following:

- **Environmental entrepreneurs** introduce new technologies and methods to help solve environmental problems. Their businesses might focus on clean energy, recycling, or **sustainable** farming and healthier foods.
- **Digital entrepreneurs** harness the power of technology. Their business might focus on creating digital products or services, or selling products online.
- **Social entrepreneurs** are interested in making changes to improve society. They start programs that help people, such as providing better food or services.

These fields can also overlap. New environmental projects can also inspire social change. Bay2Tray, for example, is a program that helps public schools that want to use local seafood. This creates healthier lunches for students and helps local business, addressing both environmental and social aspects.

Bay2Tray uses local seafood to bring nutritious meals to students.

Small Businesses, Big Effects

Many people want to become entrepreneurs and start their own businesses. Not all entrepreneurs grow their businesses into huge companies, though. Many remain small. In fact, over 90% of all companies in North America are small to medium businesses. Examples include grocery stores, laundromats, hair salons, plumbing services, and other businesses. But being small does not mean they do not have a big **impact** on their communities.

There is a **ripple effect** when a new business is created. Other businesses will spring up around the new **venture**. A dry cleaning company might help launch a delivery service. A new restaurant might help local farmers by buying their fresh meats and vegetables. One new business can help create and be supported by several other new businesses. All of these new businesses create new jobs.

When people have jobs, they also have income to spend. This is a boost for all businesses in the area, both big and small. The economy of a country runs on the strength of small business.

Small businesses are a major contributor to the strength of local economies.

A local business might run a fundraising walkathon for the community.

Small businesses can provide goods and services that bigger companies do not. These **niche industries** can improve the quality of life for everyone in the area. A gourmet dog treat company keeps local dogs happy. A market stall might sell popsicles made with juice from fresh, local fruit.

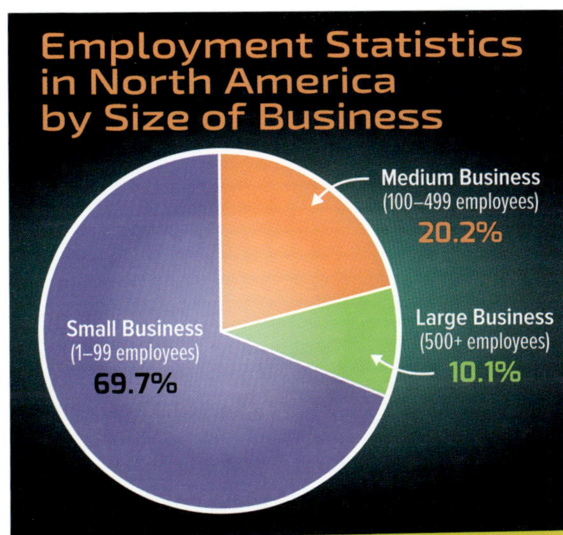

Small businesses are connected to their communities. This means they often give back in the form of donations to local charities or sponsorship of local sports teams. They can also promote causes that create social change. For example, they might support an animal shelter or start a walkathon to help raise funds for a new skateboard park.

You make the call...

Imagine you started a small business in your community. As it becomes more profitable, what local cause or social change would you hope to support? Why?

Entrepreneurs All Around You

A hockey player named Tim Horton started a successful chain of donut shops.

No matter where you live, it is almost impossible not to be affected by the work of entrepreneurs. We use their products, hire their services, and benefit from the advances they inspire in technology and protecting the environment. Sometimes the unlikeliest people turn out to be the most successful entrepreneurs.

Tim Horton, for example, was well known as a hockey player. He played for several NHL teams, including the Toronto Maple Leafs and the New York Rangers. Hockey players are not usually known for their baking skills, but Horton became forever linked with donuts and coffee. In 1964 he became an entrepreneur and opened his first donut shop in Hamilton, Ontario. It served only two products—coffee and donuts. In just three years, the business had expanded to three stores. Today there are over 3,500 restaurants in Canada, over 850 in the United States, and 56 at military stations in the Persian Gulf. They now serve a variety of drinks, baked goods, soups, and sandwiches.

Sometimes an entrepreneur can help improve lives. That is exactly what 30-year-old Michael Akindele is doing in Nigeria. Born in the United States, Akindele's parents are from Nigeria in Africa. After studying computer engineering at university, Akindele went to Nigeria. He discovered that not many people there could afford computers or smartphones, so their access to the Internet and digital content was very limited. He created a low-cost smartphone called SOLO that gives users access to millions of free, licensed songs, as well as access to movies. Akindele's company employs 160 people in Nigeria, who have a wide range of expertise, from engineering to sales. He hopes to move production of the phones from Asia to Africa soon, to create even more jobs.

Sometimes entrepreneurs just have a cool idea. At the Alamo Drafthouse Cinemas in Austin, Texas, Tim and Karrie League have become **groundbreakers** in the theater experience. For example, the action movie *The Road Warrior* will be viewed outdoors, accompanied by a live rock band and a real-life "death race." For movies shown inside the theater, staff serve made-to-order food right to moviegoers' seats.

SOLO smartphones transformed the market in Nigeria by providing more content at a lower cost than other more expensive smartphones.

2 What Does It Take to Be an Entrepreneur?

Entrepreneurs come in every age, size, background, and culture, but they share certain traits and skills. Remember that even if you weren't born with these skills, many can be practiced and improved over time.

Risk taking

Starting a new business venture can be risky. Your savings, reputation, and future might be on the line. Many entrepreneurs have to take out **loans** to fund their new business. This means being in debt, or owing money plus **interest** to the bank. If your business fails, that debt can be a burden for years.

Example

Walt Disney had nine setbacks before he became a success. At one point he had lost so much money that he had to eat dog food to survive!

Creativity

Coming up with a new or unique idea takes creativity. Entrepreneurs need to think in different ways to find solutions to common problems. Entrepreneurs think of something in their own life that is troublesome or causes them stress and unhappiness. Finding a solution to their own problem gives them ideas about how it might benefit others, too, and could be the start of a new product or service.

Example

Joy Mangano appears regularly on the Home Shopping Network with her innovative products, such as the self-wringing Miracle Mop. She became known as an inventor of practical household products. Her Forever Fragrant odor **neutralizers** broke an HSN sales record by selling over 180,000 in one day.

Morita's first product, a rice cooker, was a failure; but he kept working and eventually developed the Walkman. It has been one of the most successful personal electronics products of all time.

Flexibility

It is important for entrepreneurs to be able to react to what's going on around them. They need to be willing to change their mind at a moment's notice. When things aren't working, they need to come up with a new plan or solution. Supply problems, designs that don't work, or new competitors are all reasons to try a new strategy.

Example

Akio Morita's first attempts at making new products failed miserably. He designed a rice cooker that ended up actually burning the rice! But by changing his focus to **telecommunications**, he climbed to international success with his company, which he called Sony.

> "There's lots of bad reasons to start a company. But there's only one good, legitimate [valid] reason, and I think you know what it is: it's to change the world."
>
> —Phil Libin, CEO of Evernote, a productivity app company

Know Yourself

Many entrepreneurial skills require you to know your strengths and weaknesses, and to have the confidence and **discipline** to make changes. When you are your own boss, you are in charge of how profitable your business is and how quickly you grow.

Networking

Successful entrepreneurs learn from others. They surround themselves with experts. They ask questions. **Networking**, which is meeting and sharing information with others, helps open doors to new funding, suppliers, and customers.

Example

The hugely popular video production company Rooster Teeth got some of its inspiration by attending gaming conferences like the Electronic Entertainment Expo, or E3. There they saw the video game *The Sims 2* and got permission to use that game's world for their online show, *The Strangerhood*.

Self-confidence

When things get tough, entrepreneurs need to believe in themselves. They see challenges as opportunities. They understand that failure can be part of the process. Successful entrepreneurs will keep trying and working until they achieve their goal.

Example

Fred Smith wrote a paper for his university economics class about an overnight delivery service. His professor gave him a low mark, telling him that the idea "wasn't **feasible**." Luckily, Smith didn't listen to him and went on to establish one of the biggest overnight delivery services, which we now know as FedEx.

Self-motivation

Entrepreneurs need to have the drive to keep going in the face of problems. They need to keep learning, too. Industries, society, the environment, and technology are all constantly changing. Businesses must change, too, to keep up.

The tracking system that FedEx pioneered to help find lost packages is now used by most other carrier services.

Example

Bernard Marcus and Arthur Blank opened the first Home Depot stores after they were fired from their **retail** jobs. They took what they had learned as employees and used a warehouse system to start one of the most successful home improvement chains.

You make the call...

What do you think is the most important character trait when facing setbacks starting a new business? Explain your thinking.

Practical Knowledge

People who start businesses often have practical skills that benefit many parts of their lives, not just entrepreneurship. Being good at problem solving and money management, for example, are also useful in maintaining personal relationships and making major purchases, such as a home.

Analytical thinking

This type of thinking is the ability to break down problems into smaller, more manageable pieces. It uses logic and reason to recognize and define problems. This allows a person to organize **resources** to solve the problem and create solutions.

Example

Fahad Tariq is a graduate student at the University of Western Ontario. He was interested in starting a business that produced healthy, energy-boosting snacks. Although there are many of these snacks on the market, Tariq's analytical research showed that there was a need for lower-calorie, lower-cost snacks that his product would fill.

Money management

It is important to control costs when starting a new business. Money management skills are needed to become and stay financially successful. If a business doesn't support itself, it is a charity, not a business.

Example

Entrepreneur Michael Hyatt borrowed money to expand his business. Soon, the growth used up all the money, and the business failed. He adjusted his borrowing and spending habits and now is the co-founder and chairman of a network software company, BlueCat Networks.

Espresso bars in Italy, where people gather and talk, were the inspiration for Starbucks in North America.

Sales and promotion

It is vital to be able to explain why your product or service is a solution to a problem. Entrepreneurs **promote** their products or services with advertisements, events, or free samples.

Example

The original Starbucks sold only coffee beans and coffee-making supplies. After visiting an **espresso** bar in Italy, however, marketing director Howard Schultz decided to promote Starbucks as a "coffee bar." People were encouraged to stay, drink their coffee, and talk, like the popular pastime in Italy.

Chad Mureta: CEO of App Empire

Chad Mureta embodies many of the skills and traits of a successful entrepreneur. Bedridden after a severe car accident, he could no longer work as a real-estate agent. He still needed income to pay his huge medical bills. He started a business creating mobile apps. He has produced 46 apps so far, co-founded three app companies, and runs a blog called *App Empire*.

3 What Do I Need to Do Before Starting a Business?

Is It a Good Idea?

One of the main reasons that **start-ups** fail is because they don't offer an improved or unique product or service. But how can you tell if your idea is good enough to be profitable? You need to do some research. Examine your idea, business plan, funding, and marketing. Are these areas strong and well thought-out? If not, problems in these areas can hurt your chances for success.

- Does your idea solve a problem? The problem needs to be one that enough people really want solved.
- Is your product or service unique or innovative? If your idea has been tried before, you need to improve it somehow to put yourself ahead of the competition.
- Could others benefit from the product or service? Your potential market has to be big enough to make the business profitable.
- Will people pay for it? People spend money on products or services that solve problems for them.
- Have you tested your idea? Test it with people willing to give honest feedback and who will make up your target customers, not just on friends or family.
- Can your business grow? A good business has to have room to expand. Even if you start small, you need a plan to grow later.

Remember: If your idea is a new product or invention, it is important to check the **patent** database. A patent is a license that allows only one person or company to produce a certain invention or use a certain process for a specific length of time. That way no one can use your idea without any benefit to you. Check page 45 for links to searchable patent databases.

You make the call...

You want to create a unique product or service that gets rid of spiders inside homes. What is your product or service, and how does it benefit others? How is your product or service different from others? Who is your target group, and why would that group be willing to pay for your product or service? Think of ways that you could find people to test your product or service.

Research the Market

Andrew Hall and Jeremy Bryant wanted to have a positive impact on their community. They started Mealshare to help provide meals to young people in need.

Even if it's a good idea, your business won't be a success if you don't know your market. So what do you need to know?

- Who are the main companies in your industry? You need to know your competition, what they are doing, and what new products or services they are bringing out.
- What are the products and services already available? There is no sense in starting a business in an industry that is already **saturated** with the same product or service.
- What is new in your industry? Understanding where things are headed can lead to new ideas and opportunities and help you avoid duplicating something that is already being offered.

Andrew Hall and Jeremy Bryant:

Co-founders of Mealshare

Andrew Hall and Jeremy Bryant quit their jobs at accounting firms to launch Mealshare. Participating restaurants have items marked "mealshare" on their menus. When diners order one of these items, Mealshare also provides a hot meal to someone in need. This program is making a big impact in the communities where young people receive the meals.

Where can you find this information?

- Visit your local Chamber of Commerce. The Chamber of Commerce is a network of local business owners. They work to further the interests of local businesses and are a great source of information.

  The U.S. Chamber of Commerce Foundation helps support young entrepreneurs with its Young Entrepreneurs Academy (YEA) program. YEA is a year-long program that provides experience-based entrepreneurship programs for students in grades 6–12. In Canada, Futurpreneur Canada provides a youth mentoring program.
- Look at online government statistics, local economic development centers, or business leaders' associations. Many reports are published online and give a lot of facts and figures that paint a picture of the economy and growth in your industry.
- Look through industry directories. This will give you a great idea of the number and range of industries in your area.

Students who participate in the U. S. Chamber of Commerce Foundation's YEA Program have the opportunity to develop many of the key skills needed to be successful entrepreneurs.

Predict Market Growth

Before you start your business, you need to measure your market to know if there's room to grow. How can you do this?

- First, you need to identify your market: Will your product appeal to homeowners? Pet owners? Seniors? Families?
- Now you need an accurate count of this group in your target area. Check city records, government statistics, or business reports.

Only by knowing the size of your market can you then try to predict your company's growth by asking more questions:

- Is your market increasing or decreasing?
- By how much per year?

For instance, are more homeowners moving into the area? How many more people go online each year? Are pet sales up or down?

- What are the current prices of similar products or services in your area?
- Can you be competitive at those prices?
- Can you price lower or can you **justify** pricing higher (better quality, locally grown, organic, etc.)?

With these answers, you should have a good idea of where your business is going.

Identifying your potential customers will help you focus your marketing plan.

Assemble an Effective Team

Another important aspect of starting a business is having a good team. One person is rarely good at all tasks. Build up a network of professionals who can help you do the things you can't, such as a lawyer, accountant, banker, and so on. An entrepreneurial team will bring different talents and skill sets to the business.

The more diverse the backgrounds and skills of your team, the more creative your ideas will be when you **brainstorm** together. A group that is diverse creates **synergy**, which means the group can create more together than the individuals can alone. **Collaboration** is crucial for putting the ideas into action.

4 How Do I Prepare a Business Plan?

Why Bother?

Your business plan is the most important document you will prepare. It says who you are, describes your business and how it will operate, and shows how the business will be profitable. It is a roadmap that shows where you are going with your company. It should demonstrate that you've done your homework, understand your market, and have the potential to **generate** business.

What Should You Include in Your Plan?

A business plan is not just a page about what you want to do; a business plan consists of different parts. Each is important to help you organize and fund your business or service.

> "We are currently not planning on conquering the world."
>
> —Sergey Brin, co-founder of Google

Top Five Industries That Are Attracting Entrepreneurs

Construction

Accommodation and food services

Business services

Wholesale and retail trade

Health care and social services

Start with your business idea. Write a short paragraph that explains what industry you will be involved in, and the problem you would like to solve. How does your idea improve or benefit the industry or group of people you are targeting?

Mention your unique selling point. Explain how your product or service will be different and appeal to customers or clients. For example, your catering company could specialize in **kosher** food, which would appeal to the large Jewish community nearby.

Next, talk about your market **analysis**. Use the information you found before you started your business in terms of market evaluation, market size, and market growth. Here you could mention how many other catering companies are nearby and what type of food they serve. Research the number of Jewish residents in the wider surrounding area and how many weddings and other celebrations are held each year.

Include a SWOT analysis. SWOT stands for your company's strengths, weaknesses, opportunities, and threats. Here you could discuss the limited number of kosher items offered by other caterers, how far away the nearest competitor is, the challenge of finding reliable suppliers, or the availability of kosher chefs in your area.

You're Not Done Yet!

In your business plan, you also need to detail how your business or service will be organized. How will you pay start-up costs, how will you advertise, and how quickly will you grow?

Who's the Boss?

Website

Employees

Finances

Timeline

Summary

George Vlagos: Oak Street Bootmakers

George Vlagos's father was a cobbler, or shoemaker. He had young George work with him so that George could see how hard it was to work with your hands. He wanted to convince George to look for a different job in the future. The plan backfired. George realized instead how hard it was to find a quality pair of shoes! Now there is a six-week waitlist for one of George's designs.

Who will be in charge? Will there be an office, and where will it be set up? Here you can define your role in the catering company as a director, supervisor, or even head chef. Perhaps you have a location for your catering company that is near several rental halls and community centers.

Will there be a website? Who will create it and maintain it? These days, many companies find most of their new customers online. An attractive and easily navigated website is a big advantage. In your plan you could mention that you will include sample menus and a photo gallery of your food on your website.

Your business plan will also say whether you will have employees. The plan can specify that the business won't have employees to begin with, but with growth, that will change. If you need staff to prepare, transport, and serve your food, here you can show that you are knowledgeable about how many people you will need to run efficiently.

Financial information is critical for the success of any entrepreneurial project. How, when, and from where the **start-up money** will come needs to be thought out and written down. Is your family investing in your catering company, or have you applied for a bank loan?

A timeline is important to show that you have considered how long it may take you to reach certain milestones, such as sales targets, hiring employees, or paying back start-up loans. This is where market research comes into play. How quickly do you hope to increase the number of bookings for your catering company?

Finally, end the business plan with a short summary: include the type of activity, the unique selling point, the market to be served, the main **objectives** of the company, and any management background you have.

"I have not failed. I've just found 10,000 ways that won't work."

—Thomas Edison, inventor

5 How Do I Finance My New Business?

Finding Funds

With your business plan in place and all your market research done, you might think you are ready to open up shop. But there is one more important step. All entrepreneurial start-ups need money to begin. Even **nonprofit** organizations need some supplies to begin operations and to run promotions.

Source of Funding	Percentage of Entrepreneurs
Personal savings	77.0%
None needed	20.8%
Business loan from a bank	10.7%
Personal credit card	10.4%
Personal home equity loan	5.6%
Crowdfunding	3.0%
Loan/investment from family/friends	2.6%
Business loan from government	0.7%
Government guaranteed bank loan	0.7%
Investment by venture capitalist	0.4%

Source: U.S. Census Bureau

The chart above shows where many entrepreneurs get funding to start their businesses.

> **"** The way to get started is to quit talking and begin doing. **"**
> —Walt Disney, Disney founder

Financing is funding for a person or business venture. Finding financing is vital to starting up a business. But how much do you need and where can you find it?

It can be challenging to determine an accurate **estimate** of start-up costs, but here are some places you might find help:

- Ask other entrepreneurs in businesses like yours. Make sure these similar ventures are outside of your geographical area, though, so the person you are asking for information doesn't feel as though they are helping the competition!
- Suppliers are another good source of data. They will gladly help you with estimating costs, since they will be looking to pick up new customers.
- Almost every industry has some sort of trade association or organization that deals with businesses like yours.
- Articles in business magazines or on online news services can be a good source of information.

Common sources for funding

Once you have an idea of how much money you will need, where can you find it?

- **Personal savings:** Many entrepreneurs use money they have saved up from other jobs to start their own enterprise.
- **Friends and family:** Sometimes people close to you will lend you money or invest in your business. This is affectionately called love money. However, if your business fails, it can lead to family problems.
- **Banks:** Some banks specialize in loans to small businesses. Make sure you read all documents carefully so you understand your responsibilities and repayment details, which will include paying interest.

Investors and lenders will want to see your financial plan before offering any money for your business.

Other Ways to Find Funding

Some grants for young entrepreneurs include training and mentoring.

There are other ways to raise money. These include grants, crowdfunding, and selling **shares** in your company to investors. Each has advantages and disadvantages.

Government grants and loans

A grant is money that is given for a specific purpose and does not need to be paid back. In the United States, grants are available for nonprofit organizations and some small businesses. To be eligible, the businesses must be part of certain industries, such as manufacturing or mining. There is a searchable online database to help small businesses determine if they are eligible.

The Canadian government has several programs to help small businesses get started and grow. Some of the grants are for new businesses in specific industries, like technology, sustainable farming, and conservation. Other programs offer funding for small-business expansion.

Check page 45 for links to grant and loan databases.

Investors

Investors are people who provide money to businesses in the hope of getting part of the profit in the future. But investors are very careful about who they give their money to. Only about 5% of entrepreneurs receive funding from investors. Why is this? Many investors feel that entrepreneurs are not always ready to take their business to the next level. They worry that entrepreneurs are looking for more money because they are inexperienced in money management skills.

Dragons' Den and *Shark Tank* are two television reality shows that feature small entrepreneurs trying to persuade a panel of successful and wealthy entrepreneurs to invest in their companies. The small entrepreneurs begin their presentation with the amount of money they are asking for. They offer the investors a percentage of their business in exchange for the money. The Dragons or Sharks on the panels then ask the entrepreneurs questions to understand if the idea has a real possibility for success. Some business owners have gone on to make millions with their products or services.

Liz Bohannon is one of many small entrepreneurs who didn't get funding from the Shark Tank *investors after appearing on the program. After her appearance, however, Bohannon saw an increase in interest in her business, Sseko Sandals. Her company has received funding from other sources, and has continued to achieve success as a profitable business.*

?

You make the call...

Investors ask entrepreneurs a lot of questions before they invest funds. What questions do you think entrepreneurs should ask investors before they take their money?

6 How Do I Get My Business Running?

Who Are You?

So, you've come up with your idea, done your market research, written your business plan, and found funding. What comes next? It's time to really define who and what you are as a business.

Start by choosing a business name. This is more important than it sounds. Customers' attention can be hard to get at first. A name or **logo** that catches their attention can bring in more sales. A name that doesn't show what you do might confuse customers.

The logos for McDonald's, Google, and Apple, Inc., are three of the most recognized logos in the world. Have you seen any logos that you thought didn't work?

Target customers:

If your product is for kids, use bright colors in your logo. If your customers are adults, choose something serious.

Research the competition:

See what names have worked for the competition.

Be creative:

Make sure your business name is easy to pronounce and easy to remember, but don't shy away from making it unique.

Don't create limits:

If you use a simple name that says exactly what your business does, like Anne's Dog Treats, you limit yourself from expanding into other areas, such as cat treats.

Get feedback:

Once you've selected one or more names, ask for the opinions of friends and family. They might identify problems you didn't think of.

What about branding?

Branding means creating a name, symbol, or design that identifies a product and makes it unique. Your brand begins with your logo. Your website, labels, and promotional materials, such as flyers, postcards, and business cards, should all use your logo.

Good branding promotes **recognition**. Almost everyone knows what restaurant is represented by a giant golden "M." You know what kind of computer you are buying if the cover shows an apple with a bite out of it. Recognition means repeat customers.

> "Be undeniably good. No marketing effort or social media buzzword can be a substitute for that."
>
> —Anthony Volodkin, founder of Hype Machine, a music website

All Above Board

Before signing any contract, make sure you understand your rights and obligations.

There are a few other things you should do to protect yourself and your investment in your company.

If you are setting up a partnership with another person, you should consult a lawyer. He or she will draw up a legal contract that clearly defines how the partnership should work. If the partnership doesn't work out, there should be a plan in place for how to legally **dissolve** the partnership, as well.

If you are renting space, a lawyer should also look over any rental contracts before you sign. He or she can make sure you are protected in case of damage caused by a storm or fire, and can check the responsibilities of your landlord and procedures for complaints.

An accountant can set up a filing system for you to make tax time easier. He or she can also set up daily accounting records so you can see at a glance if you are on track with your plans or if you need to cut costs.

It is important to properly register your business. Make sure you know all the rules for doing business in your region. Check to see if your specific industry has extra regulations for health and safety.

April Glavine:

CEO of Lean Machine vending machines

Concerned about the childhood **obesity** rate in North America, April Glavine decided to do something. She wanted to change vending machines in high schools and health-care facilities. She began leasing her own vending machines with a difference—they contain only healthy snacks. She named her company Lean Machine.

April Glavine believes the snacks in vending machines like these will help students stay healthier.

Where Are You?

You will need somewhere to conduct your business. Where depends on what kind of business it is.

To keep costs down, many people run their business out of their home. This is a good option for businesses like dog walking, housecleaning, or event planning.

Online businesses can also be run from home as long as you have the proper equipment. Statistics show that 80% of people research products online before buying them, and that 50% order online —no store required.

A clean and attractive storefront offers an inviting entrance to new customers.

Other businesses require specialized locations. Any food made to be served to the public must be prepared in a commercial kitchen, not a home kitchen. There are strict rules around **sanitation**, food storage, and safety. Commercial kitchens are inspected regularly. This is a must for catering, cake decorating, or meals-to-go programs.

Auto repairs and carpentry may require special tools, equipment, and parts that need more space than is available in a home garage.

Whether you are setting up shop in your home or in another location, you need to make sure you have **business insurance**. Disaster can strike at any time, and part of running a successful business is planning ahead in case things go wrong.

Once you have your place of business, you need to promote it. A sign is important to make it easy for customers to find you and also to catch the eye of new clients. Before posting any signs for a home-based business, check rules and regulations for your area.

Gwen Jimmere: CEO and founder of NATURALICIOUS

Gwen Jimmere is the first African-American woman to have a U.S. patent for a natural haircare product. She came up with the idea after looking for a natural haircare product for herself and not being able to find one. She decided to invent her own. She also took the extra step of learning patent law, in order to save money when filing the patent.

7 What Do I Do after I Start My New Business?

What to Expect

Many entrepreneurs have a rosy view of what will happen once they start their business. They are excited about being their own boss, making their own decisions about their future, and making lots of money. But new entrepreneurs quickly realize that this new adventure comes with advantages and disadvantages.

	Advantage	Disdvantage
UPS AND DOWNS	Some days will be smooth with good sales and seeing your business grow.	Other days will be full of problems, both in and out of your control.
TIME TRIALS	As the business grows, entrepreneurs have the opportunity to set their own schedules and vacation time.	Entrepreneurs put in long hours usually for little return at the beginning.
MAKING MONEY	As a business finds its feet, the opportunity is there to make a good living or even become wealthy.	You are responsible for paying bills and employees. It can be difficult at first to make enough money to pay everyone.
CAREFUL CUSTOMERS	You have the opportunity to gain a wide customer base if your product or service is one that customers want.	People sometimes need convincing to switch brands or try something new. You will need to spend money on advertising right away to convince them to try your product or service.
HARD WORK	Seeing your hard work pay off in a strong business with good profits brings a lot of pride and self-esteem.	Being your own boss means that you need to do much of the work yourself if you don't want to spend all your profits on hiring employees.

"There's nothing wrong with staying small. You can do big things with a small team."

—Jason Fried, founder of 37signals (now called Basecamp), an app development company

Small businesses give customers more options for where to buy goods and services.

? **You make the call...**

What do you think is the biggest misconception about starting a new business? Why do you think so? What are some ways an entrepreneur could prepare to avoid this problem?

Keeping It Small

Most businesses in North America are considered small businesses. Small businesses have fewer than 100 employees. They drive our economy. Together they employ millions of workers and produce millions of products.

Small business owners face different challenges than big companies. The owners usually have to make a lot of sacrifices of their time and personal finances. To keep costs low, small companies usually employ fewer people to share the workload. Often, this means everyone has to work long hours to get the job done. On the other hand, small companies are often more flexible than larger companies and can move quickly to take advantage of sudden opportunities.

Despite the hard work, many small business owners wouldn't trade the challenges of being an entrepreneur for anything. They like having control over their own future. They know that they can celebrate every success, big or small, and it gives them a tremendous sense of personal satisfaction.

The biggest benefit for small business owners is that they are producing and offering services they believe in. They know that they are improving society, the environment, or their community.

You're Never Too Young

Creativity and innovation have no age limit. Young entrepreneurs prove that you can be successful in business if you have drive and passion. While young entrepreneurs face different challenges because of their age, many have been able to find a way around these problems and succeed.

Entrepreneurs under the age of 18 are not able to open a business bank account, be eligible for bank loans, or sign a lease. They can get around this by getting loans from family members, going into business with a trusted adult who can sign for leases and accounts, and also look into grants or funds especially for young entrepreneurs.

Young people also have the challenge of balancing work and school. Education is very important for their future and should be taken seriously. But a new business takes a lot of time and effort, so it can be difficult to find enough hours in the day for both. There are also legal restrictions about how many hours those under 18 are allowed to work per week. Young entrepreneurs can ask for help from those around them to help carry the workload and find that balance.

Moziah Bridges was disappointed at how few bow ties were available for him on the market. His grandmother helped him learn how to sew his own. He has earned over $30,000 for his bow ties so far.

Moziah Bridges likes to wear bow ties, so he started a business making them.

Jack Kim founded Benelab when he was still in high school. Benelab is a search engine that generates donations. Kim wanted to make **philanthropy** easy for everyone. He created Benelab which is a company that donates 100% of its revenue to a different charitable cause each month. Kim has established a "no adults-as-employees" rule and recruited classmates to be part of the team. Kim's goal is to reach $100,000 before he graduates from high school.

ManCan is a company that makes candles with scents targeted at men. At the age of 13, Hart Main, from Ohio, realized that men often liked different scents than women. He created a line of candles with scents such as Bacon, Coffee, New Mitt, and Grandpa's Pipe. Main got started with an investment of $100 of his own money and $200 from his parents. Today, ManCan candles are in over 60 stores across the U.S. and have sold about 9,000 units.

Juliette Brindak Blake started Missoandfriends.com when she was 16. The website is a networking site for girls only. It is aimed at tween girls and includes advice, games, and a place to connect with peers. Brindak knew the issues that tween girls face, and she wanted to help girls build their self-esteem. The site generates about 10 million monthly visits, and Brindak continues to work to find new ways to support tween girls.

Juliette Brindak Blake is the CEO of Miss O & Friends.

8 Changing the World

The business landscape is always changing. As society changes, new environmental or social problems can develop. When this happens, new opportunities arise.

Technology is one of the biggest sources of inspiration for new businesses. **Virtual reality** will become part of our everyday lives in the not-too-distant future. You'll be able to walk through a store in the comfort of your home. Some experts predict that robots will act more like our friends. A Japanese company, Softbank, is getting ready to release Pepper, its first social robot, which interacts and talks with humans.

And get ready for **wearable technology**. Smart glasses are not science fiction anymore!

All of these inventions are **fertile** ground for entrepreneurial ideas, as people look for ways to help us connect using technology in our daily lives.

Smart glasses are basically wearable computers that run mobile apps.

Think About It

1. Starting and running a new business comes with a lot of ups and downs. Often, new businesses require long hours with little time off, and many challenges can arise. What are some character traits that you feel make an entrepreneur successful, or capable of overcoming challenges? Do you have any of these traits?

2. Creating, marketing, and selling a product or service can take a lot of creativity and patience. Usually, entrepreneurs need the help of others to succeed. How could an entrepreneur make sure collaborations go smoothly?

3. A new business needs funding to help it get off the ground. What are some ways that an entrepreneur can secure funding for their business idea? Which do you feel is the most effective way to get funding? Why?

4. Small businesses make up the majority of new ventures. In what ways do small, niche businesses affect the communities that they're opened in? Think of a small business in your community. What effects does it have on the people that live there?

5. Entrepreneurs need a strong business plan to succeed in their venture. What are the different parts of a business plan? How do all of the steps connect with each other? Is one step more important than the others? Why or why not?

Next Steps

- Start now to build networks. Meet people who share your interests and passions. This will help you in the future when you need to reach out for information or advice.
- Talk to small business owners to learn which sales and marketing techniques work and which ones don't.
- Build your savings. Starting a business is expensive, and the less interest you have to pay on borrowed money, the more you will have to invest in yourself.
- Lead a volunteer effort or fundraiser. This will help you test your leadership skills as well as building your network.

Bibliography / Sources

Books

Balanko-Dickson, Greg. *Tips and Traps for Writing an Effective Business Plan*. New York: McGraw-Hill Education, 2007.

Colligan, Victoria, Beth Schoenfeldt, and Amy Swift. *Ladies Who Launch: Embracing Entrepreneurship & Creativity as a Lifestyle*. New York: St. Martin's Press, 2007.

Guillebeau, Chris. *The $100 Startup: Reinvent the Way You Make a Living, Do What You Love, and Create a New Future*. New York: Crown Business, 2012.

Kiyosaki, Robert T., and Sharon L. Lechter. *Rich Dad's Before You Quit Your Job*. Scottsdale, AZ: Plata Publishing, 2012.

Lee, Jennifer. *The Right-Brain Business Plan: A Creative, Visual Map for Success*. Novato, CA: New World Library, 2011.

Tjan, Anthony K., Richard J. Harrington, and Tsun-Yan Hsieh. *Heart, Smarts, Guts, and Luck: What It Takes to Be an Entrepreneur and Build a Great Business*. Boston: Harvard Business Review Press, 2012.

Touchie, D. *Preparing a Successful Business Plan: A Practical Guide for Small Business*. Vancouver: Self-Counsel Press, 2001.

Wilton, David, and Kyle McNamara. *Get Growing: Keys to Unlocking the Potential of Your Small Business*. Toronto: Key Porter Books, 2009.

Websites

www.entrepreneur.com

www.bdc.ca/en/i_am/young_entrepreneur/pages/default.aspx

www.iccwbo.org

www.canadabusiness.ca/eng/page/2848/

http://patft.uspto.gov/

www.uspto.gov/patents-application-process/search-patents

www.ic.gc.ca/eic/site/csbfp-pfpec.nsf/eng/Home

http://hbswk.hbs.edu/item/how-to-predict-if-a-new-business-idea-is-any-good

www.businessnewsdaily.com/7929-entrepreneurs-personal-obstacles.html

Industry Reports and Articles

Innovation, Science and Economic Development Canada. 2010. *Growth Map of Canadian Firms*. SME Research and Statistics.

Innovation, Science and Economic Development Canada. 2013. *Key Small Business Statistics*.

Peterson, R., and D. Valliere. "Entrepreneurship and national economic growth: The European entrepreneurial deficit." *European Journal of International Management* 2, no. 4 (2007): 471–490.

Valliere, D. "Why do venture capitalists make early stage investments?" *Journal of Entrepreneurial Finance and Business Venturing*, 2008.

Learning More

Books to Read

Blumenthal, Karen. *Steve Jobs: The Man Who Thought Different*. Square Fish, 2012.

Covey, Sean. *The 7 Habits of Highly Effective Teens*. New York: Touchstone, 2014.

Hoogeveen, Margaret. *What Is Social Entrepreneurship?* St. Catharines, ON: Crabtree Publishing, 2017.

Mariotti, Steve. *The Young Entrepreneur's Guide to Starting & Running a Business: Turn Your Ideas into Money!* New York: Crown Business, 2014.

Mason, Helen. *What Is Digital Entrepreneurship?* St. Catherines, ON: Crabtree Publishing, 2017.

Offord, Alexander. *What Is Environmental Entrepreneurship?* St. Catherines, ON: Crabtree Publishing, 2017.

Simmons, Michael. *The Student Success Manifesto*. New York: Extreme Entrepreneurship Education Co., 2003.

Websites to Visit

Financial knowledge and education aimed at kids:
http://kidzcountinc.org/about/

Young Entrepreneurs Academy:
http://yeausa.org/about/introduction/

Futurpreneur Canada: A national nonprofit organization that provides mentoring for aspiring young business owners:
www.futurpreneur.ca/en/about/

START-UP USA answers questions about entrepreneurship for youth with disabilities:
www.worksupport.com/documents/STARTUPQAInformationonEntrepreneurship1.pdf

The Martin Aboriginal Education Initiative teaches Aboriginal youth about business and entrepreneurship:
www.maei-ieam.ca/Aboriginal_Youth_Entrepreneurship_Program.html

U.S. Patent Database:
www.uspto.gov/patents-application-process/search-patents

Grant and loan information:
www.grants-loans.org/

U.S. Small Business Administration:
www.sba.gov/loans-grants

Glossary

analysis A detailed examination of facts

apprentice A person who is learning a trade from a skilled employer

bankrupt Unable to pay back debts

brainstorm To quickly come up with many ideas as a group without discussing or judging their merit

business insurance A financial arrangement in which a business pays a regular fee in return for money back to cover loss or damage after an accident

CEO (chief executive officer) Person, sometimes the owner, who heads a business

collaboration The act of working together

competitive Trying to be more successful than others

crowdfunding Raising money online from a large number of people

digital entrepreneurship The activity of setting up new enterprises that use online or other electronic media for all or part of the business

discipline The control and improvement of one's behavior

dissolve To officially end

economy Wealth and resources of a country or smaller area

entrepreneur Person who starts a business based on their idea

entrepreneurial process Steps that entrepreneurs take, including idea, vision, research, planning, team building, and marketing

entrepreneurship The process of turning an idea into a business

environmental entrepreneurship Starting a business by combining concern for the environment with sound business practices

espresso Strong black coffee

estimate A rough guess

feasible Possible to do easily

fertile Full of potential

generate To produce (something) or cause (something) to be produced

groundbreakers People who are leaders in a new activity

impact A strong effect

innovative Having new ideas or methods

insatiable Always wanting more

interest Fee paid for the use of someone's money, usually a percentage of the amount owed

justify To provide or be a good reason for (something)

kosher Prepared according to Jewish law

loans Money given with the expectation of repayment and payment of a fee

logo A symbol used in advertising that identifies a company

networking Meeting and sharing information with others

neutralizers Substances that act against something, making it seem as though it no longer exists

niche industries Businesses that make specific products for a small market

nonprofit Related to organizations in which making money is not the main goal of the business

obesity The state of being very overweight

objectives Goals

patent Government license granting ownership of an idea or invention

philanthropy The desire to help others, especially by a donation of money

promotion A way of increasing sales for a business

recognition The identification of something based on having seen it before

resources A supply of money or materials

retail Related to selling goods directly to customers

ripple effect The spreading consequences of one action

sanitation Cleanliness and hygiene

saturated As full as possible

shares Units of ownership of a company

social entrepreneurship The activity of setting up new enterprises with the goal of positive social impact, that is, an improvement in people's lives

start-up (*n*) a new business; (*adj*) relating to the starting of a new business

start-up money Money needed to cover the expenses of starting a new business

sustainable Refers to a system, product, or technique that can exist without doing damage to the environment; eco-friendly; green

synergy A beneficial combining of resources from different businesses, or of different people and their skills

telecommunications The technology involved in comunicating across long distances, such as radio or television

venture A risky task

virtual reality An environment that seems real but that was created by a computer

wearable technology Clothing and accessories that contain computer and electronic technology

Index

Author Biography

For many years, Natalie Hyde enjoyed running her own cottage industry. Now she writes both fiction and non-fiction books for kids. Her more than 50 non-fiction books cover topics that range from the Underground Railroad to genetics. She lives with her family in southwestern Ontario.